Unlocking Connections:

The Ultimate Guide to Mastering
Conversations with Anyone

BY

Peace J. Williams

COPYRIGHTS

Dedication

This book is dedicated to all those who strive to connect with others, embrace diversity, and foster meaningful relationships. May these pages inspire you to engage in conversations that transcend barriers and create lasting bonds.

Contents

Chapter 1: The Power of Connection. 6

Chapter 2: The Art of Small Talk......16

Chapter 3: Active Listening and Nonverbal Communication............. 25

Chapter 4: Asking Meaningful Questions..33

Chapter 5: Handling Difficult Conversations...................................40

Chapter 6: Building Lasting Connections..48

Chapter 7: Cultivating Empathy.......56

Chapter 8: Resolving Conflict Constructively...................................62

Chapter 9: Sustaining Meaningful Connections....................................68

Closing Message:.............................75

INTRODUCTION

Welcome to "Unlocking Connections: The Ultimate Guide to Mastering Conversations with Anyone." In this book, we will embark on a journey to develop the essential skills needed to engage in meaningful conversations with individuals from diverse backgrounds. Whether you're a social butterfly or an introvert seeking to enhance your communication abilities, this guide will equip you with practical techniques, valuable insights, and strategies to foster genuine connections with anyone you meet.

By embracing the power of effective communication, active listening, and understanding nonverbal cues, you will learn how to initiate conversations confidently, navigate small talk, ask meaningful questions, handle difficult conversations, and build lasting connections. Each chapter will provide actionable tips and real-life scenarios to help you put theory into practice.

As you embark on this transformative journey, remember that every conversation is an opportunity for growth, connection, and mutual understanding. By mastering the art of communication, you will unlock a world of possibilities, forge strong relationships, and leave a lasting impression on those you encounter.

We hope that "Unlocking Connections" will empower you to approach conversations with confidence, empathy, and curiosity. Now, let's begin our exploration of the fascinating world of human connection and communication.

Chapter 1: The Power of Connection

In a world where technology has made communication easier than ever, the true power of connection lies not in the devices we use but in the human interactions we cultivate. The ability to engage in meaningful conversations is a skill that transcends boundaries, builds bridges, and enriches our lives in countless ways. In this chapter, we will explore the profound impact that effective communication and connection can have on our personal and professional relationships.

1.1 Understanding the Importance of Effective Communication

Effective communication forms the foundation of successful relationships, both personal and professional. It is the vehicle through which ideas are shared, emotions are expressed, and understanding is fostered. When communication is ineffective, misunderstandings can arise, conflicts can escalate, and connections can weaken.

To understand the importance of effective communication, we must recognize its role in our daily lives. Whether it's expressing our needs and desires, collaborating with others, or building trust and rapport, communication is essential. It allows us to convey our thoughts, feelings, and intentions accurately, enabling others to understand us and vice versa.

Effective communication also enhances our problem-solving abilities. By clearly articulating our concerns, actively listening to others' perspectives, and engaging in open dialogue, we can navigate challenges more effectively and reach mutually beneficial resolutions.

Furthermore, effective communication plays a vital role in building and maintaining relationships. When we communicate authentically, openly, and respectfully, we create an environment of trust and understanding. This, in turn, strengthens our connections, fosters intimacy, and cultivates a sense of belonging.

1.2 Overcoming Barriers to Communication

Despite the importance of communication, various barriers can hinder our ability to connect effectively. These barriers may include language differences, cultural misunderstandings, physical distractions, or even internal factors like fear or insecurity.

Language barriers, for instance, can impede communication when individuals speak different languages or have limited proficiency in a shared language. In such cases, employing techniques like active listening, visual aids, or using translation services can help bridge the gap and facilitate understanding.

Cultural differences can also pose challenges to communication. Norms, values, and communication styles vary across cultures, and misinterpretations can occur if we are not aware of these nuances. By embracing cultural diversity, seeking to understand others' cultural backgrounds, and adapting our communication approach accordingly, we can foster more inclusive and effective conversations.

Physical distractions, such as noisy environments or technological interruptions, can interfere with communication. It is crucial to minimize these distractions to create a conducive environment for meaningful dialogue. Finding quiet spaces, turning off electronic devices, and actively focusing on the conversation at hand can help overcome these obstacles.

Internal barriers, such as fear, anxiety, or lack of confidence, can also hinder effective communication. These barriers may stem from past negative experiences or self-doubt. Overcoming these internal barriers requires self-awareness, self-compassion, and intentional practice. By building our confidence, managing our emotions, and developing effective communication skills, we can break through these barriers and engage in more fulfilling conversations.

1.3 Building Genuine Interest and Empathy

Genuine interest and empathy form the pillars of meaningful connections. When we genuinely care about others and seek to understand their experiences, we create an environment where authentic conversations can thrive.

Cultivating genuine interest involves active curiosity about others' lives, passions, and perspectives. It requires us to go beyond surface-level interactions and demonstrate a sincere desire to learn more about the person in front of us. By asking thoughtful questions, actively listening, and showing genuine enthusiasm, we can create a space where individuals feel valued and heard.

Empathy, on the other hand, is the ability to understand and share the feelings of others. It involves putting ourselves in someone else's shoes, acknowledging their emotions, and responding with compassion. Empathy allows us to connect on a deeper level, validate others' experiences, and foster a sense of understanding and support.

Cultivating genuine interest and empathy requires active practice. It involves being fully present in conversations, setting aside personal judgments, and embracing a non-judgmental attitude. By creating a safe space for others to express themselves authentically, we foster connections based on trust, respect, and mutual understanding.

1.4 Cultivating a Positive Mindset for Conversations

Approaching conversations with a positive mindset can significantly impact the outcomes and experiences we have. A positive mindset allows us to embrace opportunities for connection, view challenges as learning experiences, and engage with others in an open and non-judgmental manner.

Maintaining a positive mindset involves cultivating optimism, reframing negative thoughts, and focusing on the potential for growth and connection. It requires us to let go of preconceived notions, biases, and assumptions, and approach conversations with curiosity and a willingness to learn.

A positive mindset also involves embracing differences and celebrating diversity. Each person brings a unique set of experiences, perspectives, and ideas to the table. By recognizing and appreciating these differences, we can create a rich tapestry of conversations that broaden our horizons and deepen our connections.

Additionally, a positive mindset encourages us to practice gratitude and express appreciation. When we acknowledge the value others bring to our lives, we strengthen our connections and foster a culture of positivity and mutual support.

Understanding the importance of effective communication, overcoming barriers, cultivating genuine interest and empathy, and adopting a positive mindset are foundational elements for unlocking the power of connection. By honing these skills, we can create deeper, more meaningful relationships, bridge gaps in understanding, and foster an environment where authentic conversations thrive. As we continue our journey in the following chapters, we will explore practical strategies and techniques to enhance our conversational abilities and connect with anyone we encounter. Get ready to embark on a transformative exploration of the art of conversation and the limitless possibilities it holds.

HIGHLIGHTS

1. "Effective communication forms the foundation of successful relationships, both personal and professional."

2. "Cultivating genuine interest and empathy creates an environment where authentic conversations can thrive."

3. "Approaching conversations with a positive mindset enables us to embrace opportunities for connection and view challenges as learning experiences."

Chapter 2: The Art of Small Talk

Small talk serves as a social lubricant, breaking the ice and opening the doors to more meaningful conversations. While it may seem trivial, mastering the art of small talk is essential for building rapport, establishing connections, and creating a comfortable atmosphere. In this chapter, we will delve into the nuances of small talk, exploring strategies to initiate conversations, navigate through common topics, and make a lasting impression.

2.1 Mastering the Basics of Small Talk

Small talk acts as a gateway to deeper conversations, allowing individuals to connect on a surface level before delving into more significant topics. Mastering the basics of small talk involves understanding the social cues, norms, and context of different situations. It requires being aware of appropriate conversation starters, maintaining eye contact, and using open body language to convey interest and engagement.

To engage in effective small talk, it's crucial to initiate conversations with confidence and authenticity. Starting with simple, non-controversial topics such as weather, current events, or shared experiences creates a comfortable foundation. By demonstrating genuine curiosity and actively listening to the responses, we show our interest and create an environment conducive to building rapport.

Engaging in small talk also involves being mindful of our tone and delivery. A warm and friendly demeanor can make others feel more comfortable and open to conversation. By matching the energy and enthusiasm of the person we are engaging with, we create a harmonious atmosphere that encourages further interaction.

2.2 Initiating Conversations with Confidence

Initiating conversations can be daunting, especially when approaching unfamiliar individuals or entering new social settings. However, with practice and a few strategies, we can build the confidence to break the ice and start conversations effortlessly.

One key aspect of initiating conversations is having a repertoire of open-ended questions. These questions invite more detailed responses and encourage the other person to share their thoughts and experiences. By asking about someone's interests, hobbies, or opinions on a relevant topic, we can stimulate engaging conversations and show genuine interest in the other person.

It's important to be mindful of non-verbal cues, such as maintaining eye contact, smiling, and using open and welcoming body language. These non-verbal signals convey approachability and make others more likely to respond positively to our conversation initiation.

Additionally, active listening plays a significant role in initiating conversations with confidence. By attentively listening to the other person's responses and demonstrating genuine curiosity, we can respond thoughtfully and keep the conversation flowing. This not only shows respect and interest but also encourages the other person to share more about themselves.

2.3 Navigating Awkward Silences

Awkward silences can arise during small talk and can create discomfort or a sense of unease. However, they can also present opportunities for further connection and engagement. Navigating through awkward silences requires finesse and adaptability.

One effective technique to break awkward silences is to share personal anecdotes or stories related to the conversation topic. These stories add depth, provide common ground, and encourage the other person to share their own experiences. By sharing relatable and interesting anecdotes, we can create a relaxed atmosphere and invite the other person to contribute.

Using transitional phrases or open-ended prompts can also help move the conversation forward. By acknowledging the silence and introducing a new topic or asking a follow-up question, we can redirect the conversation and maintain its momentum. For example, asking about upcoming plans, recent experiences, or seeking recommendations can provide fresh avenues for discussion.

Moreover, it's important to remember that silence is not always negative. Pauses in conversations allow both parties to gather their thoughts and reflect. Embracing these moments and allowing the conversation to naturally flow can lead to deeper and more meaningful discussions.

2.4 Finding Common Ground

Finding common ground is a powerful way to establish rapport and forge connections during small talk. It involves identifying shared interests, experiences, or values that create a sense of familiarity and mutual understanding.

Active listening plays a crucial role in discovering common ground. By attentively listening to the other person's responses and asking relevant follow-up questions, we can uncover shared experiences or interests that we can further explore. This not only strengthens the connection but also shows that we value and respect the other person's input.

Being knowledgeable about a variety of topics can also facilitate finding common ground. Staying informed about current events, popular culture, or common interests allows us to engage in conversations that resonate with others and establish a sense of shared understanding. This demonstrates our willingness to connect and invest in the conversation.

Additionally, expressing genuine enthusiasm and positivity when discovering common ground helps foster a more engaging and enjoyable conversation. By highlighting shared passions or experiences, we create a bond that extends beyond small talk and sets the foundation for deeper connections.

Mastering the art of small talk is a valuable skill that paves the way for deeper connections and meaningful conversations. By understanding the basics of small talk, initiating conversations with confidence, navigating through awkward silences, and finding common ground, we can create a comfortable and engaging atmosphere for both ourselves and those we interact with. Small talk serves as a stepping stone to building rapport and establishing connections that can lead to more profound and fulfilling relationships. With practice and a genuine interest in others, we can refine this art and create lasting impressions through our conversations.

HIGHLIGHTS

1. "Mastering the basics of small talk involves understanding the social cues, norms, and context of different situations."

2. "Initiating conversations with confidence and authenticity is crucial for effective small talk."

3. "Finding common ground through active listening and shared interests builds rapport and deeper connections."

Chapter 3: Active Listening and Nonverbal Communication

Effective communication extends beyond words. Active listening and nonverbal communication play vital roles in understanding others, conveying our own messages, and building strong connections. In this chapter, we will explore the art of active listening and the power of nonverbal cues, discovering how these elements enhance our communication skills and enrich our interactions with others.

3.1 The Art of Active Listening

Active listening involves fully engaging with others and giving them our undivided attention. It goes beyond simply hearing words and requires us to be present, empathetic, and responsive. By mastering the art of active listening, we can deepen our understanding, show respect, and build meaningful connections.

One aspect of active listening is maintaining eye contact. Looking directly at the person we are conversing with conveys interest and attentiveness. It shows that we value their words and are fully engaged in the conversation.

Another important aspect of active listening is providing verbal and nonverbal cues of understanding. Nodding, using affirming statements, and paraphrasing what the other person has said demonstrates that we are actively processing their message and encourages them to share more.

Additionally, active listening involves suspending judgment and refraining from interrupting. By creating a safe and non-judgmental space for the speaker, we encourage open and honest communication. This allows the speaker to express themselves freely, fostering a deeper level of trust and connection.

3.2 The Power of Nonverbal Communication

Nonverbal communication encompasses the messages we convey through body language, facial expressions, gestures, and tone of voice. These cues often speak louder than words and significantly impact how our messages are received and interpreted.

Body language plays a crucial role in nonverbal communication. It includes posture, hand gestures, and facial expressions. Maintaining an open and relaxed posture, using appropriate gestures, and displaying facial expressions that align with our words enhance the clarity and impact of our message.

The tone of voice is another essential aspect of nonverbal communication. The way we speak, the volume, pitch, and intonation can convey emotions, attitudes, and intentions. By being mindful of our tone, we can ensure that our message is delivered accurately and that our words align with our intended meaning.

Nonverbal cues also involve being aware of the other person's body language and reactions. Paying attention to their facial expressions, posture, and gestures allows us to gauge their level of engagement, understanding, and emotional state. This awareness enables us to adjust our communication style and approach accordingly.

3.3 Enhancing Communication Through Active Listening and Nonverbal Cues

Active listening and nonverbal communication work hand in hand to enhance our overall communication skills and create meaningful connections.

Active listening enhances our understanding of the speaker's message, ensuring that we grasp their intended meaning. It allows us to respond appropriately, ask relevant questions, and show empathy and support. Through active listening, we demonstrate our respect and genuine interest in the other person's thoughts and feelings.

Nonverbal cues add depth and richness to our communication. They provide additional layers of meaning, help establish rapport, and foster understanding. By aligning our nonverbal cues with our verbal messages, we create a cohesive and authentic communication style that enhances our ability to connect with others.

Practicing active listening and being mindful of nonverbal cues require conscious effort and continuous improvement. By honing these skills, we become more effective communicators, deepen our relationships, and create a positive and inclusive communication environment.

Active listening and nonverbal communication are powerful tools that enrich our communication abilities. By mastering the art of active listening, we demonstrate respect, understanding, and empathy. Incorporating nonverbal cues such as body language, facial expressions, and tone of voice allows us to communicate more effectively and create deeper connections with others. By practicing active listening and being aware of nonverbal communication, we enhance our overall communication skills and pave the way for more meaningful and fulfilling interactions.

HIGHLIGHTS

1. "Active listening involves fully engaging with others, giving them our undivided attention, and creating a safe space for open and honest communication."

2. "Nonverbal communication, including body language and tone of voice, plays a significant role in conveying messages and influencing how they are received."

3. "By mastering active listening and being mindful of nonverbal cues, we can enhance our overall communication skills, deepen understanding, and create more meaningful connections."

Chapter 4: Asking Meaningful Questions

Asking meaningful questions is an essential skill for effective communication. Thoughtful and well-crafted questions not only demonstrate our curiosity and interest in others but also facilitate deeper conversations and understanding. In this chapter, we will explore the art of asking meaningful questions, understanding different question types, and using them to foster meaningful connections.

4.1 The Power of Thoughtful Questions

Thoughtful questions have the ability to unlock insights, encourage reflection, and stimulate engaging conversations. They go beyond surface-level inquiries and delve into deeper thoughts, emotions, and perspectives. By asking thoughtful questions, we can build rapport, demonstrate empathy, and create a space for authentic and meaningful exchanges.

Thoughtful questions are open-ended, allowing the person to respond with more than a simple "yes" or "no." They invite detailed responses, encouraging individuals to share their experiences, opinions, and feelings. By asking questions that require more than a brief response, we show our genuine interest and provide an opportunity for the speaker to express themselves fully.

Furthermore, thoughtful questions foster active listening. When we ask thought-provoking questions, we are more inclined to listen attentively to the responses, seeking a deeper understanding of the speaker's perspective. This promotes a respectful and engaging dialogue, enhancing the overall quality of the conversation.

4.2 Different Types of Meaningful Questions

There are different types of meaningful questions that we can utilize depending on the context and purpose of the conversation. Each type serves a unique function in eliciting specific information or encouraging reflection.

Exploratory questions aim to uncover new information and perspectives. They encourage individuals to share their thoughts, experiences, and ideas in a more comprehensive manner. Examples of exploratory questions include "What led you to that conclusion?" or "Tell me more about your thought process."

Reflective questions prompt individuals to examine their own thoughts and feelings. They encourage introspection and self-awareness. Reflective questions often start with phrases like "How do you feel about...?" or "What impact did that have on you?"

Empathetic questions show genuine care and understanding. They allow us to express empathy and support. Examples of empathetic questions include "How are you coping with that?" or "What can I do to support you?"

Challenging questions invite individuals to critically think and analyze different perspectives. They encourage deep reflection and can stimulate meaningful discussions. Challenging questions often start with phrases like "Have you considered the implications of...?" or "What alternatives have you explored?"

4.3 Building Connections Through Meaningful Questions

Asking meaningful questions is a powerful tool for building connections and establishing trust. By demonstrating genuine curiosity and active listening, we create an environment that encourages open and honest communication.

Meaningful questions help us uncover common interests, values, and experiences, fostering a sense of shared understanding. They provide an opportunity to explore topics that matter to both parties, creating a foundation for deeper connections and more meaningful relationships.

Moreover, meaningful questions show respect for the other person's thoughts and perspectives. They validate their experiences and emotions, creating a sense of validation and trust. By asking questions that go beyond the surface, we signal our interest in their unique experiences and viewpoints.

Asking meaningful questions is a valuable skill that enhances our communication abilities and strengthens our connections with others. Thoughtful and well-crafted questions demonstrate our curiosity, foster active listening, and create space for deeper conversations. By understanding different question types and utilizing them appropriately, we can engage in meaningful exchanges that promote understanding, empathy, and authentic connections. By incorporating meaningful questions into our communication repertoire, we enrich our interactions and create a more meaningful and fulfilling communication experience.

HIGHLIGHTS

1. "Thoughtful questions stimulate engaging conversations and foster meaningful connections."
2. "Different types of questions, such as exploratory, reflective, empathetic, and challenging, serve unique functions in eliciting specific information or encouraging reflection."
3. "Asking meaningful questions demonstrates curiosity, promotes active listening, and builds rapport and trust with others."

Chapter 5: Handling Difficult Conversations

Difficult conversations are an inevitable part of life, and mastering the art of handling them is essential for maintaining healthy relationships and resolving conflicts. In this chapter, we will delve into strategies and techniques for navigating difficult conversations with empathy, assertiveness, and respect. By developing effective communication skills during challenging situations, we can foster understanding, find common ground, and work towards mutually beneficial outcomes.

5.1 Preparing for Difficult Conversations

Preparing oneself before engaging in a difficult conversation is crucial for achieving a positive outcome. Taking the time to reflect on the issue at hand and identifying the desired outcome can help set the stage for a productive dialogue.

Firstly, managing our emotions is essential. Emotions can easily escalate during difficult conversations, so it's important to find healthy ways to regulate them. Engaging in self-care activities, such as deep breathing exercises or practicing mindfulness, can help us stay calm and centered before entering the conversation.

Additionally, clarifying the purpose of the conversation and setting realistic expectations is beneficial. Considering different perspectives and potential solutions beforehand allows us to approach the conversation with a balanced mindset. This preparation helps us remain focused and open to alternative viewpoints.

5.2 Active Listening and Empathy

Active listening and empathy are fundamental skills for handling difficult conversations. By actively listening to the other person's perspective and seeking to understand their point of view, we create an atmosphere of respect and trust.

Empathy involves putting ourselves in the other person's shoes and genuinely understanding their emotions and experiences. It requires suspending judgment and actively striving to grasp their feelings. By acknowledging their emotions and validating their experiences, we create a safe space for open and honest communication.

Active listening techniques, such as paraphrasing, summarizing, and asking clarifying questions, help ensure that we fully understand the other person's thoughts and feelings. This not only demonstrates our engagement but also enables us to address their concerns more effectively.

5.3 Assertiveness and Respectful Communication

Assertiveness plays a vital role in difficult conversations. It involves expressing our thoughts, needs, and boundaries clearly and respectfully, while also remaining receptive to the other person's perspective.

Using "I" statements allows us to express our feelings and opinions without sounding accusatory or judgmental. By focusing on our own experiences and avoiding generalizations, we encourage a more constructive dialogue.

Respecting the other person's point of view, even if we disagree, is essential in maintaining a productive conversation. Engaging in active and open-minded discussion, rather than resorting to defensive or confrontational behavior, creates an atmosphere conducive to finding common ground.

Furthermore, nonverbal cues can enhance our assertiveness and demonstrate that we value the conversation and the other person's input. Maintaining eye contact, using open body language, and adopting a calm and composed demeanor convey our engagement and willingness to listen.

5.4 Finding Common Ground and Seeking Solutions

In difficult conversations, the ultimate goal is often to find common ground and seek solutions that satisfy both parties. By focusing on shared interests and common goals, we can identify areas of agreement and work towards mutually beneficial outcomes.

Active problem-solving techniques, such as brainstorming or exploring alternative options, can help generate creative solutions and move the conversation forward. This collaborative approach fosters a sense of partnership and encourages both parties to contribute to the resolution process.

When faced with obstacles or disagreements, it is important to remain flexible and open to compromise. By maintaining a respectful and solution-oriented mindset, we increase the chances of finding mutually acceptable resolutions.

Handling difficult conversations requires a combination of empathy, active listening, assertiveness, and respect. By preparing ourselves mentally, actively listening with empathy, and communicating assertively and respectfully, we can navigate difficult conversations with greater ease and effectiveness. By seeking common ground, engaging in problem-solving, and remaining open to compromise, we can find resolutions that promote understanding, preserve relationships, and foster growth and positive outcomes.

HIGHLIGHTS

1. "Preparing oneself mentally and emotionally is crucial for navigating difficult conversations effectively."

2. "Active listening and empathy create an environment of trust and understanding during challenging dialogues."

3. "Assertiveness and respectful communication are essential in finding common ground and seeking mutually beneficial solutions."

Chapter 6: Building Lasting Connections

Building lasting connections is a valuable skill that enriches our personal and professional lives. Meaningful relationships contribute to our overall well-being and open doors to new opportunities. In this chapter, we will delve into strategies and techniques for nurturing and maintaining lasting connections with others. By understanding the principles of building relationships, practicing effective communication, and investing time and effort, we can foster connections that stand the test of time.

6.1 Authenticity and Vulnerability

Authenticity forms the bedrock of building lasting connections. Being true to ourselves and expressing our genuine thoughts and emotions allows others to see and connect with the real us. When we embrace our uniqueness and share our authentic selves, we attract people who appreciate us for who we truly are.

Authenticity starts with self-awareness. It requires us to explore our values, beliefs, and passions, and align our actions and communication with them. When we are authentic, we emit a sense of honesty and genuineness that resonates with others. People are drawn to those who are comfortable in their own skin and aren't afraid to show their true selves.

Vulnerability is also a key aspect of building lasting connections. It involves being open and willing to share our fears, hopes, and challenges with others. When we allow ourselves to be vulnerable, we create opportunities for deeper understanding, empathy, and connection. Sharing our vulnerabilities encourages others to reciprocate, fostering a sense of trust and mutual support.

Being vulnerable requires courage and trust. It means stepping out of our comfort zone and revealing our authentic selves, even when it feels uncomfortable. Vulnerability allows us to forge deeper connections and build relationships based on authenticity and mutual understanding.

6.2 Effective Communication

Effective communication is a vital component of building lasting connections. It encompasses both listening and expressing ourselves clearly and respectfully.

Listening attentively to others demonstrates that we value their thoughts and opinions. It requires us to be present in the moment, giving our full attention to the person speaking. Active listening involves not only hearing the words but also understanding the underlying emotions and intentions. It means paying attention to nonverbal cues, such as body language and facial expressions, which can provide valuable insights into the speaker's emotions.

Expressing ourselves clearly and respectfully is equally important. Effective communication involves conveying our thoughts, feelings, and needs in a way that others can understand. It requires us to choose our words carefully, ensuring that they accurately reflect our intentions and are considerate of the other person's feelings.

Using assertive communication techniques, such as "I" statements, allows us to express ourselves honestly without being aggressive or passive. By using "I" statements, we take ownership of our thoughts and emotions, creating a safe and non-blaming environment for open dialogue. Assertive communication fosters understanding, reduces misunderstandings, and promotes healthy interaction and connection.

6.3 Investing Time and Effort

Building lasting connections requires time and effort. Relationships flourish when nurtured and given attention.

Investing time means prioritizing relationships in our lives. It involves actively engaging with others, spending quality time together, and showing genuine interest in their lives. Meaningful connections require regular interaction and ongoing communication. Whether it's scheduling regular catch-up sessions, planning activities together, or simply checking in to see how someone is doing, investing time is crucial for building and maintaining strong connections.

Putting effort into relationships means going beyond surface-level interactions. It entails showing support, being available during challenging times, and celebrating each other's successes. It means being a good listener, providing a shoulder to lean on, and offering assistance when needed. Effort also involves showing empathy and understanding, being patient and forgiving, and being willing to compromise and work through difficulties together.

Additionally, being proactive in maintaining relationships is essential.

It involves initiating contact, planning social gatherings, and taking an active role in staying connected. Proactivity demonstrates our commitment to the relationship and shows that we value the connection. It means reaching out to friends, family, and colleagues, even when life gets busy, and making an effort to keep the relationship alive.

Building lasting connections is a lifelong journey that requires authenticity, effective communication, and investment of time and effort. By embracing our true selves, practicing active listening, expressing ourselves clearly and respectfully, and nurturing relationships with care, we can cultivate connections that endure. These lasting connections enrich our lives, provide support and companionship, and contribute to our overall happiness and fulfillment. By prioritizing and investing in meaningful relationships, we lay the foundation for a life filled with meaningful connections and lasting impact.

HIGHLIGHTS

1. "Authenticity forms the foundation for building lasting connections."

2. "Vulnerability creates opportunities for deeper understanding and trust in relationships."

3. "Effective communication, both listening and expressing oneself, is vital for nurturing connections."

Chapter 7: Cultivating Empathy

Empathy is a powerful tool that enhances our ability to build meaningful connections with others. It involves understanding and sharing the feelings and perspectives of those around us. In this chapter, we will explore the significance of cultivating empathy and how it can strengthen our relationships. By developing our empathetic skills, we can create deeper connections, foster understanding, and promote harmony and compassion in our interactions.

7.1 Understanding Empathy

Empathy is a multi-faceted concept that goes beyond surface-level understanding. It requires us to truly put ourselves in someone else's shoes and experience the world from their perspective. To cultivate empathy, we need to develop self-awareness and mindfulness.

Self-awareness plays a pivotal role in empathy as it involves recognizing and regulating our own emotions. When we are more aware of our own emotional state, we are better equipped to approach others with an open and non-judgmental mindset. By acknowledging and understanding our own emotions, we become more attuned to the emotions of those around us.

Mindfulness is another essential aspect of cultivating empathy. It involves being present in the moment and fully attentive to the experiences and emotions of others. By practicing mindfulness, we can overcome distractions and actively engage with others, demonstrating our genuine interest in their well-being.

7.2 Practicing Active Listening

Active listening is a fundamental component of empathy. It requires us to give our full attention to the speaker, not only listening to their words but also paying attention to their body language, tone of voice, and emotions. Through active listening, we can create a safe and supportive space for others to express themselves.

To practice active listening, we should strive to be fully present in the conversation. This means eliminating distractions and focusing our attention solely on the speaker. By maintaining eye contact, nodding to show understanding, and using verbal and nonverbal cues, we communicate that we are actively engaged and genuinely interested in what the speaker is saying.

Additionally, it is important to suspend judgment and refrain from interrupting. By allowing the speaker to fully express themselves without interruption, we validate their experiences and emotions. Active listening fosters a sense of trust and creates an environment where individuals feel heard and understood.

7.3 Cultivating Empathetic Responses

Active listening lays the foundation for cultivating empathetic responses. Empathetic responses involve acknowledging and validating the emotions of others, providing comfort and support, and showing understanding and compassion.

One effective way to cultivate empathetic responses is through reflective listening. Reflective listening involves paraphrasing and summarizing the speaker's words to ensure that we accurately understand their perspective. This technique allows the speaker to feel heard and encourages further exploration of their thoughts and feelings.

In addition to verbal responses, nonverbal cues play a significant role in expressing empathy. Simple gestures such as nodding, smiling, and maintaining an open and welcoming body posture can convey our empathy and create a safe space for the other person to share their emotions.

Cultivating empathy is a valuable skill that enhances our relationships and fosters deeper connections with others. By understanding and sharing the emotions of those around us, we create an environment of compassion, understanding, and support. Through self-awareness, mindfulness, active listening, and empathetic responses, we can cultivate empathy and enrich our interactions with others. Cultivating empathy not only benefits our relationships but also contributes to a more compassionate and empathetic society as a whole.

HIGHLIGHTS

1. "Empathy involves understanding and sharing the feelings and perspectives of others."

2. "Active listening is crucial for cultivating empathy and creating a safe space for others to express themselves."

3. "Cultivating empathetic responses, such as reflective listening and nonverbal cues, fosters understanding and validates the emotions of others."

Chapter 8: Resolving Conflict Constructively

Conflict is a natural part of any relationship, and knowing how to resolve it constructively is essential for building lasting connections. In this chapter, we will delve into strategies for managing and resolving conflicts in a healthy and productive manner. By developing conflict resolution skills, we can address differences, find common ground, and maintain strong and resilient relationships even in the face of challenges.

8.1 Understanding Conflict

Conflict arises when there are differing opinions, needs, or values between individuals or groups. It is important to understand that conflict itself is not inherently negative. It can be an opportunity for growth, understanding, and positive change if managed effectively.

To effectively resolve conflict, it is crucial to recognize and acknowledge its presence. This involves identifying the underlying issues, emotions, and perspectives of all parties involved. By understanding the root causes of the conflict, we can begin the process of resolution.

8.2 Effective Communication in Conflict Resolution

Effective communication is a cornerstone of resolving conflicts constructively. It enables us to express ourselves clearly, actively listen to others, and find mutually acceptable solutions.

When engaging in conflict resolution, it is important to communicate assertively and respectfully. This means expressing our thoughts, feelings, and needs in a clear and non-confrontational manner. By using "I" statements and avoiding blame or criticism, we create a safe and open environment for dialogue.

Active listening is equally important during conflict resolution. It involves giving our full attention to the other person, seeking to understand their perspective, and validating their emotions. By actively listening, we demonstrate empathy and show a genuine willingness to find common ground.

8.3 Collaborative Problem-Solving

Collaborative problem-solving is a key approach to resolving conflicts constructively. It involves working together to find mutually beneficial solutions that address the concerns of all parties involved.

In collaborative problem-solving, it is essential to focus on interests rather than positions. This means understanding the underlying needs, motivations, and values that drive each party's position in the conflict. By identifying shared interests and exploring creative solutions, we can find outcomes that satisfy everyone involved.

Additionally, maintaining open and honest communication throughout the process is vital. This includes being willing to compromise, seeking win-win solutions, and fostering a sense of cooperation and respect. By emphasizing collaboration and problem-solving, we can transform conflicts into opportunities for growth and stronger relationships.

Resolving conflict constructively is a crucial skill for building and maintaining healthy relationships. By understanding conflict, practicing effective communication, and engaging in collaborative problem-solving, we can navigate disagreements and differences in a way that strengthens our connections with others. Conflict resolution allows us to address issues, find common ground, and foster understanding and empathy. By approaching conflict with a constructive mindset, we can transform challenges into opportunities for growth, learning, and stronger bonds.

HIGHLIGHTS

1. "Conflict presents an opportunity for growth and positive change if managed effectively."

2. "Effective communication, including active listening and assertive expression, is crucial in resolving conflicts constructively."

3. "Collaborative problem-solving focuses on shared interests and finding win-win solutions to address the concerns of all parties involved."

Chapter 9: Sustaining Meaningful Connections

In this final chapter, we will delve into the essential strategies for sustaining and nurturing meaningful connections. Building strong and lasting relationships requires ongoing effort, effective communication, and a commitment to mutual growth. By cultivating certain habits and attitudes, we can ensure that our connections remain vibrant, fulfilling, and resilient over time.

9.1 Nurturing Relationships

Nurturing relationships goes beyond the initial stages of connection and involves actively investing time and energy into fostering growth and maintaining the bond. It requires continuous communication, support, and a genuine interest in the well-being of the other person. To nurture relationships effectively, it is important to express appreciation and gratitude, as these acts of kindness reinforce the value we place on the connection. Additionally, being there for others during both joyful and challenging times fosters a deep sense of trust and strengthens the emotional connection.

In nurturing relationships, it is vital to prioritize active and empathetic listening. By truly understanding the thoughts, feelings, and needs of the other person, we create an environment of validation and understanding. Regular check-ins and open conversations also play a crucial role in nurturing relationships, as they allow both parties to share their joys, concerns, and aspirations. By maintaining consistent and meaningful communication, we show our commitment to the connection and create a space where both individuals feel safe and valued.

Furthermore, nurturing relationships involves engaging in shared activities and creating positive memories together. By actively participating in experiences that both individuals enjoy, we deepen the bond and create a reservoir of shared experiences. These shared activities can range from simple moments of laughter and conversation to more significant adventures or projects. The key is to prioritize quality time and create opportunities for connection and growth.

9.2 Managing Boundaries

Managing boundaries is an essential aspect of sustaining healthy relationships. Boundaries help define personal space, emotional limits, and acceptable behavior within the connection. Open and honest communication is crucial in establishing and maintaining boundaries. It is important to express our needs, desires, and limits clearly and respectfully. By doing so, we create a foundation of trust, respect, and understanding.

Respecting the boundaries of others is equally vital. It requires actively listening to their needs and desires, and adapting our behavior accordingly. Respecting boundaries demonstrates empathy, sensitivity, and a genuine desire to honor the autonomy and well-being of the other person. It is essential to recognize that boundaries may evolve over time, and ongoing communication and flexibility are key to managing boundaries effectively.

In addition to individual boundaries, it is important to establish shared boundaries within the relationship. These shared boundaries may involve agreements on aspects such as privacy, personal goals, and mutual responsibilities. By jointly defining and respecting these boundaries, both individuals contribute to a healthy and harmonious relationship dynamic.

9.3 Continuous Growth and Learning

Sustaining meaningful connections requires a commitment to continuous growth and learning. This involves personal development, self-reflection, and a willingness to adapt and evolve alongside the relationship. Each individual brings their unique experiences, perspectives, and aspirations to the connection, and it is through growth and learning that we foster mutual understanding and appreciation.

Engaging in continuous growth and learning within the relationship involves being open to new experiences and ideas. It requires a curiosity and willingness to explore different viewpoints, challenge assumptions, and expand our understanding of the world. By actively seeking out new knowledge, engaging in personal development activities, and embracing lifelong learning, we bring freshness and vitality to the connection.

Self-reflection is another essential aspect of continuous growth. Taking the time to introspect and evaluate our own thoughts, feelings, and behaviors allows us to gain insights into how we contribute to the relationship. Self-reflection helps us identify areas for personal growth, recognize patterns or triggers that may impact the connection, and make necessary adjustments to enhance the relationship dynamics.

HIGHLIGHTS

1. "Nurturing relationships requires continuous communication, support, and a genuine interest in the well-being of the other person."
2. "Managing boundaries involves open and honest communication, respecting personal space, emotional limits, and establishing shared boundaries within the relationship."
3. "Continuous growth and learning are essential for sustaining meaningful connections, involving personal development, self-reflection, and a willingness to adapt and embrace new experiences."

Closing Message:

Dear Reader,

Thank you for embarking on this transformative journey with me through the pages of this book. Throughout our exploration of effective communication, connection-building, and relationship management, you have gained valuable knowledge and skills that can make a profound difference in your interactions and connections with others.

By delving into the power of connection, the art of small talk, active listening, meaningful questioning, handling difficult conversations, building lasting connections, cultivating empathy, resolving conflicts constructively, nurturing relationships, managing boundaries, and embracing continuous growth and learning, you have equipped yourself with a toolbox of communication strategies that can enhance the quality of your relationships.

As you reflect on the contents of this book, I invite you to recognize the significance of the topics covered. Effective communication and meaningful connections are not just essential skills; they are the foundations upon which we build fulfilling and harmonious relationships in all aspects of our lives. By mastering these skills, you have the power to positively impact your personal and professional relationships, foster understanding and empathy, and create a more connected and compassionate world.

I want you to take a moment to appreciate the value you have gained from reading this book. The insights, techniques, and perspectives shared within these pages are tools that can empower you to navigate social interactions with confidence, build strong connections with others, and experience the joy and fulfillment that come from meaningful relationships. The investment you have made in your personal growth and communication skills is an investment that will continue to pay dividends throughout your life.

Now, armed with this newfound knowledge, it is time to put it into practice. Embrace every opportunity to engage in meaningful conversations, to truly listen and understand others, and to nurture the connections that matter most to you. Remember, meaningful connections are not created overnight; they require time, effort, and genuine care. But the rewards they bring are immeasurable—deep friendships, supportive networks, and a sense of belonging and fulfillment.

As you close this book, carry with you the belief that you have the power to connect with anyone, to make a positive impact through your words and actions, and to cultivate relationships that enrich both your life and the lives of those around you. Embrace the challenges and opportunities that lie ahead, knowing that your journey toward better communication and meaningful connections has just begun.

Thank you for joining me on this enlightening voyage. I am confident that the knowledge and skills you have acquired will serve you well in your personal and professional interactions. Remember, the connections you forge can change lives, including your own. So go forth with confidence, compassion, and the commitment to building lasting and meaningful connections.

Wishing you a future filled with enriching relationships and the joy that comes from connecting deeply with others.

Yours Faithfully,

Peace Williams

OTHER BOOKS BY THE SAME AUTHOR

1. ADHD Cognitive Behavioral Therapy (CBT)
2. Social Anxiety Solutions
3. Mastering ADHD
4. Mastering Anger
5. Confidence Unleashed
6. Resilient Minds: Empowering Recovery With DBT Skills
7. ADHD workbook for Women
8. Acceptance and Commitment Therapy (ACT) for ADHD
9. Breaking Free: A Journey to Recovery from Narcissistic Abuse
10. The Powerful guide to DBT skills
11. Self-love Workbook for Black Women
12. DBT for Anxiety

Printed in Great Britain
by Amazon

25102797R00046